Return To Me

What if God hates religion?

Tiffany Holcomb

WestBow Press
P R E S S
A DIVISION OF THOMAS NELSON

WestBow Press books may be ordered through booksellers or by contacting:

WestBow Press
A Division of Thomas Nelson
1663 Liberty Drive
Bloomington, IN 47403
www.westbowpress.com
1-(866) 928-1240

Because of the dynamic nature of the Internet, any web addresses or links contained in this book may have changed since publication and may no longer be valid. The views expressed in this work are solely those of the author and do not necessarily reflect the views of the publisher, and the publisher hereby disclaims any responsibility for them.

Certain stock imagery © Thinkstock.

ISBN: 978-1-4497-1394-2 (sc)
ISBN: 978-1-4497-1395-9 (e)

Library of Congress Control Number: 2011923714

Printed in the United States of America

Scripture quotations marked are taken from the Holy Bible, New Living Translation, copyright 1996, 2004. Used by permission of Tyndale House Publishers, Inc., Carol Stream, Illinois, 60188. All rights reserved.

Scripture taken from the Holy Bible, New International Version. Copyright 1973, 1978, 1984 by International Bible Society. Used by permission of Zondervan. All rights reserved.

Scripture taken from The Message. Copyright 1993, 1994, 1995, 1996, 2000, 2001, 2002. Used by permission of NavPress Publishing Group.

WestBow Press rev. date: 3/11/2011

For My Sweet Savior Jesus, the Lover of my soul.

Thank You for the cross.

Thank You for Your Faithfulness.

Thank You for the gentle nudges in my life.

You complete me. I cannot wait to see You face to face!

Contents

Introduction

From generation to generation there has been absence to the truth of the character of God. He has been misunderstood, mistreated and portrayed as a wrath filled being that is waiting to zap us all into hell. This has been a great lie from the enemy and he has had great success in spreading the news both in the world and in the church. My prayer is that God would be known for who He truly is not what you have heard about Him but who He really is. He loves ALL the people that He created with a deep and passionate love. There is story after story in the Old and New Testament of His relentless pursuit after those He created. It is so essential that you read the bible for yourself from cover to cover to discover who the One True God is.

If we look around at America we see nothing but pride and greed. We find our right to express our feelings as long as they are politically correct. We are very full of ourselves. We are "the whatever feels good we should do it" generation. Whatever we think is best for us is what we will do. We are falling apart at the seams. We are losing our way and our culture is heading downhill fast.

If we look at the church today well we just blend in with the rest of the world. We go through the motions of church and we fill our lives with empty religion. We carry around our "holey" bible. We have taken out what we don't want to be obedient to and have changed some of the rules to make it fit into our lives. We as the church have become very judgmental of one another because if we are focused on what other people are doing wrong then we can escape what we are doing wrong. Unfortunately we are a mirror to the Israelites. They were God's chosen people and we as the church are God's chosen people but when things don't seem to go the way that we think they should well we start to make up our own rules. We start to go down paths that were never meant for us to travel down. We start to reason away what the TRUTH is and we compromise the Word of God for what makes us comfortable. This is not what God had in mind for the church.

The church has actually turned people away from God. There are people who call themselves Christians and they are the most selfish people I have ever met. Christians everyday are turning people away from Jesus. We have heard the prosperity gospel and the good works gospel. We have turned people away from the faith when they have SINNED instead of loving them through their SIN. We tend to get caught up in the religious expectations that we have of each other. We need to take a look at the way that Jesus encountered people in sin. He was more interested in the care and transformation of the sinner than He was in the sin and the requirements of the law. We have become an organization that does things in the name of Jesus but we don't act like Jesus. We have become empty religion. Jesus never called anyone to a religion only into a relationship with Him. We have created our own way to heaven. We think that the better we are the easier the way to heaven. We have made it about baptism, confirmation, church attendance, how we worship on Sundays and acts of service. We get into the comparison game of how we are serving the Lord versus how he/she serves the Lord. We are all different. He has us exactly the way He wants us. God just wants our hearts and to come to Him just as we are. We are broken people in need of a Savior to save us from whatever it is that we struggle with.

I don't know what may have distorted your view of God and Jesus. Maybe your own expectations of how your life should have turned out or someone else's view of God got in the way of you getting to know Him on your own. There is always something in this world that will pull you away from a loving and forgiving God.

Jesus loved on everyone. Jesus loved the alcoholics, the addicts, the prostitutes. He hung around the thieves and the liars. He wasn't looking for a group of people that He could become like He was looking for the person that He could change from the inside out. We as the church have it all wrong. We have gotten caught up in all of our programs and religious festivals and God HATES it! God does not hate you He hates religion!

Amos 5:21-24 The Message

I can't stand your religious meetings. I'm fed up with your conferences and conventions. I want nothing to do with your religion projects, your pretentious slogans and goals. I'm sick of your fund-raising schemes, your public relations and image making. I've had all I can take of your noisy ego-music. When was the last time you sang to ME? Do you know what I want? I want justice-oceans of it. I want fairness-rivers of it. That's what I want. That's all I want.

God has been stirring this message in my heart for quite some time now to RETURN TO HIM. We have gotten so caught up in our empty religion and going through the motions of being a Christian that we have forgotten about the relationship with Him. Jesus wants us to have a deep, intimate, growing to become more like Christ everyday relationship. We have forgotten that when we fall down Jesus is there to pick us up. We have missed that His Grace is enough for us. We have lost our way and turned to idols to get us through our day. We go to everyone and everything before we go to the One who is more than enough for any need or desire that we may have. From Genesis to Revelation God is chasing His children and begging them to RETURN TO HIM. He wants nothing more than to be in our lives.

Wandering in the Desert

Deuteronomy 6:5 The Message Love God, your God, with your whole heart: love Him with all that is in you, love Him with all that you've got.

Expectation: the act or the state of expecting or something expected; a thing looked forward to.

Everyone has expectations for their life. We place high expectations on our self, our marriage, our kids, our friends, our careers and our God. Most of the time life does not turn out to be anything like the expectations that we had planned for our lives. What happens when we have placed our lives in God's hands and our expectations don't turn out like we had planned? What happens when we have trusted God to make our dreams come true and they are just not matching up? We begin to wander in the desert and we allow our hearts to wander. We start to wander into our way of thinking and we start to doubt that God can do what He says He can do. We begin to rely on our own understanding of things instead of trusting that God knows what is best for me and for you. *Proverbs 3:5 NIV Trust in the Lord with all your heart; do not depend on your own understanding.* We allow doubts, disappointments and distractions to take the place of God.

1

Circumstances also make our hearts wander away from God. When your husband decides He doesn't want to be married anymore and leaves you with the children, the house and the bills. You lost the perfect job that you have put your whole life into and the bills are piling up. You get the call from the doctor and you hear the news that you have cancer and it really doesn't look good for you. Your house has been stolen to foreclosure. Our children are going astray. Every time we turn on the news there is another violent crime of rape and child molestation which has touched many of us personally. Poverty and homelessness is increasing daily. Abortion has become our birth control and the list goes on and on.

We live in a fallen world and if we live defined by the circumstances that we endure than we will live a defeated life. Our whole life we will come up against circumstances in our lives. There is always going to be a trial to overcome. Jesus said in *John 16:33 NIV I have told you these things so that in me you may have peace. In this world you will have trouble. But take heart I have overcome the world.* We have planted this idea in our heads that with God in our lives everything is going to work out. The plans that we make will work out because God is good. We tend to forget His Words or we have not taken the time to get to know His Words. Jesus said, "In Me you will have peace" not in this world you will have peace. He said, "In this world you will have trouble." He warned us we would have troubles and trials. He never said to make all your plans and I will follow you or I will make sure you fulfill them. *Jeremiah 29:11 NIV For I know the plans that I have for you, "declares the Lord, "plans to prosper you and not to harm you, plans to give you a hope and a future.* He has good things planned for our lives and that means they are His things planned for our lives not ours and this is where we need to surrender our lives to Him. When trials or trouble come we should be drawing as near to God as we can. Instead of choosing to go against what God has planned we need to go with Him.

Circumstances and unmet expectations cause our hearts to wander. Wander means to stray from a path, place or companion without a fixed plan. Heart means the center of the total personality or the innermost central part of anything. When we put these two together we have the innermost part of us straying from place to place without a fixed plan. This is exactly what happens to each of us when our expectations are not met. We all have wandering hearts at times. When I look around the church today it is filled with wandering hearts. It is not only the church but it is the world we live in filled with wandering hearts. We can all get so easily distracted by our circumstances that we end up leaving our fixed plan. For those of us who have already made Jesus the Lord of our life He is to be the center of our hearts. Jesus is our fixed plan and for those of you who have not met Jesus yet my prayer is that He will be your fixed plan by the end of this book. Whether you have had an encounter with Jesus or not we have one thing in common and that is that our hearts wander. This is why it is so important that we fix our plan on Jesus Christ.

At some point in our lives we have had an expectation of God. Somewhere in your life you made up your mind about who God is and what He is like. You may have been influenced by someone else's bad experience with God. It may not have been a bad experience with God but maybe a bad experience of church. Either one has made you search no more. Somewhere in your own walk things did not go the way you thought they should have and you became enslaved to disappointment. You didn't like the answer that He gave you. He closed the door to that relationship that you wanted so badly. You expected to have children by now and the test is negative once again. Your husband has left you and is not coming back. He found someone new. Your child has gone astray or has become addicted to drugs. The perfect opportunity for our hearts to wander is when we have unmet expectations and circumstances do not turn out the way we planned. We start to focus on ourselves and our hurt. We had an expectation of Jesus and He did not meet it and so we start to wander.

I often think of David when I think of a wandering heart and yet God called him a man after His own heart. When he was after God's heart he did God things. He defeated the giant Goliath with just a sling and a stone. He was the greatest King of Israel and defeated many armies that were against him. When David chose to look at his circumstances his heart began to wander and he found himself consumed in a life of adultery and murder. He easily became a liar and betrayal became natural to him. He overlooked the sins of his children and chose to not discipline them.

When David was looking at his circumstances his heart wandered. He was well into being King and becoming very successful in defeating the lands around him. David became focused on his own desires and his own plan. He strayed away from the purpose and plan that God had for him by staying home from the war. David could not sleep and wandered from his bed to his rooftop and saw a beautiful woman bathing on her roof top and instantly his heart wandered to lust. He inquired of her and before he knew it they were committing adultery. David allowed himself to wander into temptation and the consequences were devastating.

It is when we take our eyes off of our fixed plan, Jesus and put our eyes on the things of this world that our hearts begin to wander. We begin to focus our attention and depend on people or material possessions to make us happy or to complete us. Just like David when we go after the things of this world our world falls apart. Today we are just like David. We get bored when we are not seeing God in our everyday lives. We are so busy that we don't spend time with Jesus which gives us plenty of time for our hearts to wander because they are not being filled by Jesus. Our plans take precedent over God's plan.

Our hearts are prone to wander. We start to look at our circumstances or our unmet expectations and we open the door to our wandering heart. We begin to allow our thoughts of discontent to take over our thoughts of contentment in Jesus. We start to focus on all of the temporary things of this world instead of the eternal things that will last forever. We tend to forget Matthew 6:33 to seek first the kingdom of God and all these things shall be added unto you and we focus on our self and what we want right now.

One of my favorite stories from the Old Testament is the deliverance of Israel from Egypt to freedom. They were enslaved to Pharaoh and the Egyptians for 400 years. They were cruelly oppressed. They prayed to God for deliverance. God heard their cries and He chose Moses to be their leader. They were miraculously delivered from the Egyptians. God revealed Himself over and over again by protecting them from the plagues and rescued them out of Egypt with the miracle of the Red Sea. *Exodus 14:31 NLT When the people of Israel saw the mighty power that the Lord had unleashed against the Egyptians, they were filled with awe before Him. They put their faith in the Lord and in His servant Moses.* They are celebrating their victory in song and dance praising the Lord. Three days later after traveling through the desert with no water they start to realize their circumstance that they have no water. They have expectations that they will be well taken care of and enter the promised land of milk and honey IMMEDIATELY! They reach some water and it is bitter, they cannot drink it. They start grumbling to Moses. Moses cries out to the Lord with their problem and God provides a piece of wood to sweeten the water and they drink. The Lord says to them, in *Exodus 15:26 NIV If you listen carefully to the voice of the Lord your God and do what is right in His eyes, if you pay attention to His commands and keep all His decrees, I will not bring any of the diseases I brought on the Egyptians for I am the Lord who heals you."* They are content only temporarily when their needs are being met.

Just a few days later we find them grumbling again saying that they would have been better off dying in Egypt than being delivered into the desert away from their bondage and slavery. Their expectation was not met so they chose to look back on what once was. Even though they were slaves in Egypt they knew what was expected of them. They had pots of meat and ate all the food that they wanted. They were torn between two lives. They had a life full of bondage and dependence on people that they preferred over a life of freedom with dependence on God. They continually chose to focus their attention and their attitudes on their circumstances and their unmet expectations which lead them on a 40 year journey through the desert. A journey that should have only taken 11 days, amazing isn't it? But we do the same thing, don't we? We accept the new life that Jesus offers us as a better place to spend eternity but we seem to stay in the comforts of our own slavery while we wait for the promise of eternity. Our expectations were not met so we become comfortable in the pain of our husband walking out on us and starting a new life. We lost our beautiful house with the white picket fence and have allowed our financial burdens to doubt that God will provide. We have just gotten the call from the doctor that its cancer and we can't seem to find it in us that God has a plan even if cancer is a part of it.

We have an enemy and he is very aware of our ways of dealing with things. His name is Satan. We often think of him as an angry little devil dressed in red with his pitchfork in hand. He is not a little devil by any means. He has studied us humans for a long time and he is cunning and manipulative and He knows exactly how to get to us. He does not poke us with a pitchfork. He attacks us in our minds. He knows that when we are in unmet expectations or unusual circumstances that he can cause us to doubt God. He loves to distract and destroy. He puts the ideas in our minds to allow our hearts to wander. He does not want us to look at our lives through an eternal view but only a temporary view. He wants us to take our eyes off of our Creator and focus on the creation and love the things of this world. We are in the battle. It is part of your journey with Jesus. Life is full of choices and God has written out a plan in His Word for our lives. We will choose to follow God's voice or the enemy's voice. God told the Israelites to listen carefully to the voice of the Lord your God and He has the same message for us today. We need to get into His Word and know when it is His voice and not the enemies. We can so easily get caught up in our own little world blaming God for all that is wrong in it. We are not willing to take that step of faith to believe that God has a plan for our lives no matter what the circumstance is. It is time to stop depending on expectations from people or expectations about ourselves! We have to change the way we think about God. We need to get to know His Heart and after we begin to know His Heart we can begin to understand His Plan for our lives.

When I was a kid I loved to watch cartoons. One of my favorites was the coyote and roadrunner. They were constantly at war with each other and the roadrunner always won. That coyote could not get ahead of that roadrunner. He often had the expectation that he was going to win but never did. In almost every episode he would end up broken and bruised and slowly rise up his white flag of surrender. It is time to start raising your white flag of surrender. So before we go any further it is time to lay down our expectations of our life and while we are at it lay down those expectations that you have placed on the people in your life. How about today starting the most exciting adventure in your life? If you have already asked Jesus to come and dwell in your heart and have confessed Him as Lord of your life then today you have the opportunity to invite Him into every part of your life, to give yourself to Him completely and surrender all? If you have not asked Jesus into your heart and into your life then today is your day! You will not regret this decision EVER! Just say a little something like this, Jesus I want you to be in my life every day. I acknowledge that you died on the cross for me and my sin and you paid the price for me so that I could be free from the power of sin. I want to fall in love with you and get to know you in a deep and personal way. Thank you for loving me with your unfailing love. In the Mighty Name of Jesus! Amen!

Does God hate me?

≫≪

Micah 6:8 NIV And what does the Lord require of you? To act justly and to love mercy and to walk humbly before your God.

Unfortunately God has been given a bad name. Religion has given Him a bad name. I cannot tell you how many times I have heard people express the question, "Does God hate me?" Why is my life so bad? Once again we allow our circumstances to tell us who God is and if He loves us or not.

God is not into RELIGION. He never has been into religion. He has always been into having a relationship with His kids. You and me we are His kids.

Luke 15:11-25 The Message then He said," There was once a man who had two sons. The younger said to his father, "Father I want right now what is coming to me."

So the Father divided the property between them. It wasn't long before the younger son packed his bags and left for a distant country. There undisciplined and dissipated he wasted everything he had. After he had gone through all of his money, there was a bad famine through that country and he began to hurt. He signed on with a citizen there who assigned him to his fields to sop the pigs. He was so hungry he would have eaten the corncobs in the pig slop, but no one would give him any.

That brought him to his senses, He said, "All those farmhands working for my father sit down to three meals a day and here I am starving to death. I'm going back to my father. I'll say to him Father I've sinned against God, I've sinned before you; I don't deserve to be called your son. Take me on as a hired hand." He got right up and went home to his father.

When he was still a long way off, his father saw him. His heart pounding, he ran out, embraced him, and kissed him. The son started his speech: Father, I've sinned against God. I've sinned before you; I don't deserve to be called your son ever again.

But the Father wasn't listening. He was calling to the servants, "Quick. Bring a clean set of clothes and dress him. Put the family ring on his finger and sandals on his feet. Then get a grain fed heifer and roast it. We're going to feast! We are going to have a wonderful time! My son is here-given up for dead and now alive! Given up for lost but now is found! And they began to have a wonderful time!"

We have all been that prodigal child! We want right now what we want. We want the money to live out the lavish lifestyle of the American Dream. We want the white picket fence to surround the big house. We want the nice cars and we want the nice clothes. We want to stay looking youthful so we get whatever surgery that will help us accomplish that! Unfortunately some of us will do whatever it takes to get that look or that stuff. Some of us know the Father and some of us don't but that doesn't stop us. We want what we want and we want it now. Because of God's grace and mercy on us He allows us to go through the motions of our wanting. He allows us to go ahead and make mistakes just like this father did with his son. Our big problem is that most of us don't come to the great realization that God may have allowed us to make our own mistakes but the consequences are ours to deal with as well. The Prodigal Son came to his senses when he was being forced to live in ways that even the servants from his home did not have to. He didn't blame his dad for allowing him to have his inheritance. He realized it was his choices that led to his consequences. I have heard too many people struggle with the why question. Why did God allow this to happen? The answer almost always with a few exceptions has to do with a human's choice whether yours or someone else's that left a consequence. Look back on your life and notice when you have felt the farthest away from God it is usually after you have chosen to sin.

Did God hate the prodigal son? There could not be a clearer picture of who God is and what He is all about. The father in this story is our heavenly Father. He is ALWAYS on the search for us. No matter where we go, He follows us. He is such a gentleman and allows us to come back to Him. He will not push His way back into our lives. He waits for us. He knows every detail of our lives. He knows the number of hairs on our head and down to the number of breaths we will take before we spend eternity with Him.

God just like the father in this story is not mad at you. He is watching ready to run to you when He sees that you are ready to come home and have the party of your life. Notice this father did not rub his son's mistakes in his face or even bring up the past. That is exactly what our God is like. He doesn't want to revisit old neighborhoods that did nothing for us but fill us with shame and guilt. He wants to us to return to Him and receive the free gift of forgiveness and mercy. Are you ready to come home to your loving Father?

Prodigal means recklessly extravagant, luxuriant or profuse. This can be both a positive and a negative. We see both sides in the parable of the Prodigal son. The son had a negative prodigal where God had a positive. The Prodigal son went and was recklessly extravagant in a wasteful way. He took all that he had and wasted it all with nothing to show at the end. God was and is recklessly extravagant with His love. There is no limit to His love.

He is always waiting and anticipating when the wandering child will come home. He loves us with a reckless kind of love. He doesn't put limits on it.

1 Corinthians 13:4-8 NLT Love is patient and kind. Love is not jealous or boastful or proud or rude. It does not demand its own way. It is not irritable, and it keeps no record of being wronged. It does not rejoice about injustice but rejoices whenever the truth wins out. Love never gives up, never loses faith, is always hopeful, and endures through every circumstance.

1 John 4:16 says that God is love which would make God all of this. God never gives up on anyone! God cares more for others than for self. God doesn't strut. God doesn't have a swelled head. God doesn't force Himself on others. God isn't always "me first". God doesn't fly off the handle. God doesn't keep score of the sins of others. God doesn't revel when others grovel. God takes pleasure in the flowering of truth. God always looks for the best. God never looks back. God keeps going til the end.

He is patient with us. He does not push His way into our lives but allows us to go through our life making our own choices whether they are His Will or not. He waits for us to realize our need for Him. He is slow to anger and just longs for us to get to know Him in the same way that He knows us. He knows when we are awake and when we are asleep. He knows what our favorite color is and what the desires of our heart are. He created you in the image of Him so if you are crazy about music, sports or jumping out of an airplane there is a little bit of God's character there. We have a great and mighty God that deserves all the praise and glory!

If there is one thing that I have discovered in my walk with God is that God meets us where we are at and He accepts us no matter what shape we are in. He doesn't care where you have been or what you have done all He cares about is after you have that encounter with Him where you go from there.

God accepts us where He finds us but He is not going to leave you in that mess and that is where Jesus comes in. There is a huge gap between who God is and who we are. God is holy and perfect and we are broken, hurt and full of sin. Some of us are really good people but we still have a whole lot of sin. Jesus is the gap filler. He fills in that gap between who God is and who we are. Jesus is holy and perfect and yet He became broken, beaten beyond recognition and our sin consumed Him while His body hung on the cross. Jesus is the only thing that we need to make us right with God. What we do and how many times we attend church has nothing to do with where we stand with God. This is where you are going to need to have faith. *1 Corinthians 1:18 NIV For the message of the cross is foolishness to those who are perishing, but to us who are being saved it is the Power of God.* The world has made getting into heaven about us. It has nothing to do with us and has everything to do with Jesus.

There is nothing more important than knowing who God really is. What and how we think about God will affect every other decision we make. It is not easy to understand who God truly is. We will be on a lifelong adventure discovering new things about God. The more we know about God the more we grow to love Him.

We have all made poor choices. Along with those choices we have had to deal with the consequences. We never went to God to find out what He would have chosen for us, but somehow the mess we have gotten ourselves into becomes His fault. We don't like it when things don't turn out the way that we think they should so we blame God and we get mad at Him. We refuse to walk with Him anymore but what amazes me is that we never went to God to see how He would have had us do it to begin with. God wants to be a part of your life everyday! He does not want us to wait until we get to heaven to have an intimate daily relationship with Him. God already knows every detail of your life. Your days are numbered. He created you exactly the way that you are. He is passionate about being in your life.

For many years I thought all wrong about God. I thought that I could never measure up to God's standards. I was constantly trying to do good things to make my way to God's heart. I thought God was always angry at me and that He was waiting for me to do something wrong so that He could wash His Hands of me. I thought it was me and my choices that made up God's mind about me. I thought that it was my acts of kindness that allowed God to love me. I just thought of Him as the Creator of the world and the Righteous Judge who was waiting to sentence me to hell for all that I have done wrong. I often would get caught up in my guilt and shame and run as far away as I could get from Him. I thought all those things because someone else put those thoughts in my mind. Religion put those things in my mind. I would have never found the true character of God had I gone on trusting in someone else's views of God or trusting in man made religion. That is why it is so important that we get to know Him for who He truly is so that we can experience Him and have a relationship with Him. *Isaiah 46:3-4 NLT I created you and I have cared for you since before you were born. I will be your God throughout your lifetime-until your hair is white with age. I made you and I will care for you. I will carry you along and I will save you.* I love how often God calls Himself *YOUR GOD.* He is a personal and intimate God that wants to be YOUR GOD. That doesn't sound like a distant impersonal God. He has cared for us since before we were born and He will be our God throughout our lifetime. He doesn't tell us that He will be our God until we stray off the path with Him or until we mess up. He says that He will be our God throughout our lifetime. He doesn't give up on us. He knows we will wander and He allows us to make our own choices.

Psalm 139:2 NLT says You know when I sit down and when I stand up. You know my every thought when far away Psalm 139:3b NLT You know everything that I do. Psalm 139:17 NLT says How precious are your thoughts about me O God! They cannot be numbered.

He knows us like no one else will ever know us. He knows everything about us. There is nothing that we can hide from Him. He took great detail in creating each one of us. He knew every step we would take even when they were in the direction away from Him. He didn't decide to erase us or stop creating us He continued to love us. He knew that when we did step away that He would be right there waiting for us when we realized what it was like to be without Him.

Our God is a good God and He is good all the time. There are things that we are just not going to understand this side of eternity of things that happen to us and to our loved ones but that is where our faith kicks in and we believe that God has a good plan for our lives no matter what!

Psalm 107 is a great illustration of how good God is. In Psalm 107:4-9 He talks about how we will wander away from Him but as the wanderer calls out the Lord rescues them. Psalm 107:17-20 talks about a distressed people. We become distressed when we are in rebellion to God and fighting against Him and His commandments. But if we call out to Him He rescues us. Everyone is distressed right now. Our world is more unstable than it has ever been. We are not financially secure and we are distressed. Cry out to God and allow Him to be your comfort and your rescue. Psalm 107:23-30 tells us about the storm tossed. Are you storm tossed? Been in some trying times for a long time now feeling a little battered and bruised? Call out to Him and He will rescue you. Rest in His Goodness and know that there is nothing that can separate you from His Love.

We have an amazing God and I want to share with you a story from the Old Testament that truly changed my view of God. It is found in Exodus 33:18-23. It is the story of Moses asking to see God in His Glory. I think of how good God is every time that I read this. I often run to this scripture when I am struggling with my faith. We just cannot handle all of God's goodness. His goodness is revealed in His mercy, His grace, His compassion, His faithfulness, His forgiveness and His justice. Moses has been obedient. He has done what God has asked Him to do but He wants to see God. He wants more of God. He wants to see Him with his eyes. So Moses asks God to show him His glory. Reveal yourself to me. God replies with I will make all of My goodness pass before you but you cannot look directly at My face because you won't live. The compassion and love that we see in the Lord as He wants to give to His child what he has asked of Him is truly amazing to me. He always wants to give us the desires of our heart but He also knows what will be good for us and what will harm us even when we think we can handle it. God tells him stand here on this rock BESIDE ME. Does it get any more personal than that? He doesn't tell him to move away from Him He tells Him to move closer right next to Him so He could protect him and catch him if he fell. As I pass by I will hide you in a rock so that you don't get hurt and then I will cover you with My hand as I pass by until I have gone past and then when it is safe I will remove My hand and you can take a look at the back of Me. He knows what we can handle and what we can't handle and no one has been able to see the face of God and live.

He has unfailing love for us. Unfailing means certain, reliable and steadfast. He is certain that He loves us. He is reliable in His love for us. There is nothing that can separate us from His Love. *Romans 8:38 NLT And I am convinced that nothing can ever separate us from God's Love. Neither death nor life, neither angels or demons, neither our fears for today nor our worries about tomorrow- not even the powers of hell can separate us from God's Love.* The day that Jesus hung on the cross we were all on His mind. Christ died while we were still sinners. No matter where we have been or what we have done His Love endures and is unfailing. Divorce, drug addiction, adultery, abortion, cancer, bankruptcy, foreclosure, child abuse, rape, rejection it doesn't matter His Love covers it.

God is a redeemer. He makes all things new. He is in the restoration business and whatever it is that you have lost He will restore it. The one thing we need to remember is that we may never get back the exact thing that we lost but He will fill that void with something far better. In this day and age we just throw everything away when it is broken or not working like we think it should but God does the opposite He uses our old broken stuff in our lives and makes them new. God gave us Jesus so that He could make up for all of our faults and shortcomings and make us NEW in Him.

Now that you have a glimpse of God I pray that you are ready to surrender to Him. He has been chasing after you your whole life waiting for the time that you would let go and surrender to Him. Allow Him to be your loving Father and walk with Him the rest of the days of your life.

Removing the Mask of Religion

*Mark 7:6-8 NLT Jesus replied, "You hypocrites!
Isaiah was right when he prophesied about you,
for he wrote, These people honor me with their
lips, but their hearts are far from me. Their
worship is a farce, for they teach man-made ideas
as commands from God. For you ignore God's
law and substitute your own tradition."*

A mask is a disguise over a true feature. In other words a cover up for what is really going on.

Just like we have all created this picture of who we think God is we all have created different masks that we wear so that people will like us and will accept us. Underneath our masks we are a bunch of broken, messed up people. We want to look like the one with the strong emotional side so we put on the mask of never being hurt before. We put on the mask of success so that no one would ever know that we have failed. Some of us wear a mask of belonging so we can become like a chameleon and turn into whatever the crowd looks like around us so that we are accepted and not left out. We put on the mask of religion so that we can look good on the outside when really we are working our way right into a self-righteous way to God.

People have been running away from God because of religion. I have been walking with the Lord for 12 years now. I have been involved with the Christian church for 12 years. I look at the church and I see a lot of religion going on. I see a lot of Pharisees and religious leaders rising up. I have fallen into the trap of religion myself. Our flesh wants to follow religion because it makes us feel safe. The better we do religion the more God loves us which could not be farther from the truth. God doesn't have a scale that weighs our good deeds and bad but most of us with our mask of religion believe this lie.

What we do makes God love us. Lie. What Jesus did on the cross allows God to love us when we accept Jesus because His blood washes our sin. Truth.

Religion is about how you get baptized, how and when you take communion, if you raise your hands to worship or not, altar calls, confessionals and how you use your spiritual gifts. Religion is about rules and opinions of different groups of people that believe different things.

Religion makes you work your way to God but God has already paved a way straight to our hearts through Jesus. That's all that is needed.

Religion is about control, guilt and shame. When you follow a religion you will allow that religion to control you through guilt and shame of never measuring up to its expectations. It will constantly weigh you down with its burden. Religion is a burden. The religious leaders did it back in Jesus day and our religious leaders do it today.

Religion is judgmental and full of pride. Religion gives people the authority to judge your life. Religion will judge you.

Religion will never let you come as you are. *Jesus Christ said, "Healthy people don't need a doctor-sick people do. I have come to call not those who think they are righteous but those that think they are sinners."* Jesus is gentle and humble.

Religion becomes a barrier to God. The right way to approach God is simply to receive His grace with humility and gratitude and be honest about who you are before Him.

Religion has nothing to do with Jesus. Jesus is our only connection to God. Jesus is the way to get to heaven. So today are you ready to remove your mask of religion? Are you ready to come as you are no matter what that means for you and learn to live each day wholly surrendered to Jesus?

There are two stories in the gospel of Luke that will help us remove our mask of religion. The first is found in

Luke 18:9-13 The Message He told His next story to some who were complacently pleased with themselves over their moral performance and looked down their noses at the common of people. "Two men went up to the Temple to pray, one a Pharisee, the other a tax man. The Pharisee posed and prayed like this: 'Oh God, I thank you that I am not like other people-robbers, crooks, adulterers, or heaven forbid, like this tax man. I fast twice a week and tithe on all my income.' "Meanwhile the tax man, slumped in the shadows, his face in his hands, not daring to look up, said, 'God give mercy. Forgive me, a sinner.'"

The Pharisees were a religious/political party that held a conservative view of the bible. The tax collector was the enemy because he agreed to work for the Roman government to collect his own people's money to give to the Roman officials who ruled over Israel in Jesus' day.

The Pharisee with his mask on of religion had the outer looking really good. He was posed when he prayed. He had all the outer good deeds shining. He was claiming the great deeds he did in the name of God. He fasted, he prayed and he tithed all his income. He was good on the outside. He was judging this tax collector. He was comparing their lives to God.

The tax collector on the other hand was face down eating dirt holding his head in his hands disgusted with himself. He was broken. He was looking at his heart and realizing that it was only God's mercy and grace that could help him now. He was humbled by God not because of what God did to Him but because of who God is.

The temple was a place where the people could go and pray. The Pharisee had no intention of praying. He went to show off his spiritual pride. The tax collector on the other hand went to find God for forgiveness and healing of his sin.

Psalm 51:16-17 NIV You do not delight in sacrifice, or I would bring it; you do not take pleasure in burnt offerings. The sacrifices of God are a broken spirit; a broken and contrite heart, O God, you will not despise.

Psalm 51:16-17 The Message Going through the motions doesn't please You, a flawless performance is nothing to you. I learned God worship when my pride was shattered. Heart-shattered lives ready for love don't for a moment escape God's notice.

Luke 18:14 The Message Jesus commented, "This tax man, not the other went home made right with God. If you walk around with your nose in the air, you're going to end up flat on your face, but if you're content to be simply yourself, you will become more than yourself."

Jesus told the crowd that day that it was the dirty tax collector that went home and was right with God. Jesus was not into the outer religious acts. It is time to remove our mask of religion and realize our heart shattered lives before God. He is interested in our brokenness so He can fix it. He wants to mend our shattered heart but this can only happen when our pride is shattered. We need to realize that our selfish acts of righteousness are no longer needed in order for us to be made right with God. These acts do nothing for God when our hearts are not completely His. He wants a humble heart that is looking for Him. He wants a heart that hurts when it sins. He doesn't need another religious heart to show off what it does in His Name.

Luke 7:36-50 The Message One of the Pharisees asked him over for a meal. He went to the Pharisee's house and sat down at the dinner table. Just then a woman of the village, the town harlot, having learned that Jesus was a guest in the home of the Pharisee, came with a bottle of very expensive perfume and stood at His feet, weeping, raining tears on His feet. Letting down her hair, she dried his feet, kissed them and anointed them with the perfume. When the Pharisee who had invited Him saw this, he said to himself, "If this man was the prophet I thought He was, he would have known what kind of woman this is who is falling over Him."

Jesus said to him, "Simon, I have something to tell you."

"Oh? Tell me."

Two men were in debt to a banker. One owed five hundred silver pieces, the other fifty. Neither of them could pay up, and so the banker cancelled both debts. Which of the two would be more grateful?

Simon answered, "I suppose the one who was forgiven the most."

"That's right," said Jesus. Then turning to the woman, but speaking to Simon, he said," Do you see this woman? I came to your home, you provided no water for my feet, but she rained tears on my feet and dried them with her hair. You gave me no greeting, but from

the time I arrived she hasn't quit kissing my feet. You provide nothing for freshening up, but she soothed my feet with perfume. Impressive, isn't it? She was forgiven many, many sins, and so she is very, very grateful. If the forgiveness is minimal, the gratitude is minimal."

Then He spoke to her, "I forgive your sins."

That set the dinner guests, talking behind his back: "Who does He think He is, forgiving sins?"

He ignored them and said to the woman, "Your faith has saved you. Go in peace."

Once again when you compare the sinners and the religious leaders the sinners are accepted by Jesus and the religious leaders are rebuked. In Jesus day there were customs that were followed when you entered someone's home. A kiss on each cheek was a common greeting at the time. They all wore sandals in those days so the washing of feet or at least some water offered to you to wash the dust off your feet would be there upon your arrival. I can only assume but since Simon did neither of these leads me to think that he must have thought of himself as better than Jesus. That is what religion creates. It makes us think what we do is better than who God is.

Jesus once again removed the mask of religion and showed mercy, grace and love to the sinner. Are we free enough from religion to take off our mask of religion and approach Jesus like this sinful woman did? Can you freely come to Him just as you are and bring yourself to Him with your brokenness and allow Him to cleanse you from the inside out? This sinful woman did not care what people thought about her especially the religious leaders she just knew she had to show Jesus the love she felt for Him for His forgiveness of her many, many sins! It is when we realize the depths of God's forgiveness that we will take off our mask of religion and rain our tears of worship down on His feet!

Encounters with Jesus

≈

*Matthew 11:28-30 NLT Then Jesus said, "Come
to me all of you who are weary and carry heavy
burdens, and I will give you rest. Take my
yoke upon you. Let me teach you, because I am
humble and gentle at heart, and you will find
rest for your souls. For my yoke is easy to bear,
and the burden I give you is light."*

Throughout the New Testament there is story after story of
encounters between people and Jesus. When I began to read
in Matthew I fell in love with Jesus. I could not believe that
the Creator of the universe chose to come down to earth and
become like us. He could have chosen to come down and
experience life with every need met. He could have been born
in a palace and had servants meet His every need but He chose
to be born in a barn with stinky animals around. He chose a
teenager, an ordinary girl to do an extraordinary job of being
His earthly mother. His step-father was an average guy whose
job was a carpenter and they struggled to make ends meet just
like most of us. He had sibling rivalry and struggled with all
the things that we would struggle with. Anger, lust, gossip,
longing for what other people had, doubt and insecurity were

just a few of the daily struggles. He had to struggle with it but by His reliance on the Father He lived this life without sin. He had the flesh ripped off His back so that we would be healed and He suffered the insults and mockery of the Roman soldiers. He was spit on and beaten down with words. He was beaten beyond recognition as a human being. People that saw Him after His beating did not even recognize Him as a man. The flesh on His body was ripped off of Him. He was whipped over and over and over. He endured much pain. He had a crown of thorns forced into His temples. His hands and feet were pierced with a stake driven through them to hold His body up on a cross and He died a horrible death of crucifixion. He did it for you. He did it for me.

Amazing isn't it? His love is amazing. Our God endured death for us. So our God came here to us and paved the way for us to spend eternity with Him in a perfect world forever. That perfect world without pain and tears. That perfect world that was always on His mind from creation would be ours to live in forever, if only we would believe. That is all that is required of us, is to believe in Jesus Christ the Savior of the World. Sounds so simple and so many people are going to spend eternity in hell separated from God because of their pride and their choice to not believe in a God that loves them with an unending love, He loves them enough that He suffered and died for them.

Mark 5:24-34 NLT Jesus went with him, and all the people followed, crowding around Him. A woman in the crowd had suffered for twelve years with constant bleeding. She had suffered a great deal from many doctors, and over the years she had spent everything she had to pay them, but she had gotten no better. In fact she had gotten worse. She had heard about Jesus, so she came up behind him through the crowd and touched His robe. For she thought to herself, "If I can just touch His robe, I will be healed." Immediately the bleeding stopped, and she could feel in her body that she had been healed of this terrible condition.

Jesus realized at once that healing power had gone out from Him, so He turned around in the crowd and asked, "Who touched my robe?"

His disciples said to Him, "Look at this crowd pressing around you. How can you ask, 'Who touched me?'"

But He kept on looking around to see who had done it. Then the frightened woman, trembling at the realization of what had happened to her, came and fell to her knees in front of Him and told Him what she had done. And He said to her, "Daughter, your faith has made you well. Go in peace. Your suffering is over."

I don't know what her name was but I do know that she had been broken and beaten up physically and emotionally. This is a woman who knew suffering well. She had not stopped bleeding for 12 years. In those days because she had been bleeding she was unclean which meant she could not interact with anyone. As an unclean woman she was not welcome in society. She was an outcast. She would have been ignored by everyone. If she had children they were taken from her. If she was married she would have been rejected by her husband and he probably divorced her. She knew in the depths of her soul what it meant to feel lonely.

She was exhausted. She went from doctor to doctor to find a cure only to be left with her bleeding more. She had spent every penny she had just trying to get better. She was lonely, hopeless and poor. She was forced to live on the outskirts of town away from everyone. She would have been uninvited to any family gatherings. She could never walk into the temple to pray. She was exhausted emotionally and physically.

She must have heard a lot of commotion and many voices calling on the name of Jesus to save them and heal them from their diseases. "Jesus, please heal my daughter, she is very ill!" "My friend is paralyzed and cannot walk please come and heal him." "Jesus I have been blind since birth please help me to see!" Shouts of despair crying out from everywhere in such desperation. None were as desperate and lonely as her though. She realized that Jesus was her only hope. He was her answer. He could set her free from this disease that held her captive and alone. She got up enough courage to push her way through the crowd. She couldn't let her problems or what people thought of her get in the way of running to Jesus. If only I could touch His clothes I would be healed. She didn't want to be seen or noticed. She only wanted to blend in with the crowd for once. She reaches out and touches the back of Jesus and immediately her bleeding stops. She feels alive for the first time in 12 years. She chose to run to Jesus instead of running away from Him and her bleeding stopped and she was free. But just her physical healing wasn't enough for Jesus, Jesus wanted her to be healed emotionally too. He knew the depths of rejection that scarred her heart. He knew that loneliness had become a normal feeling to her. He felt the power leave His body to heal her. He stopped and asked Who touched my clothes? I can just see her kneeling on the ground trying to blend in with the crowd wishing she could remain unnoticed and He says it again who touched me? She knew it was her that He wanted. She stepped towards him trembling with fear. She fell at His feet waiting to hear those familiar words of rejection. Jesus did not want to reject her He wanted to set her free from her suffering and He did. She needed a Savior and she found Him. As she kneels at His feet head hung low she is waiting for the rejection to begin and the shouts to start coming from the crowd, unclean, unclean she is unclean. But she hears the most amazing voice speak to her, Daughter your faith has made you well. Go in peace. Your suffering is over!

As much as the bleeding woman wanted to go unnoticed because that had become comfortable for her Jesus wanted to make sure that she was noticed. He wanted to make her feel accepted and loved. He wanted her to know that her suffering was over. I think He wanted the crowd to see that this "unclean" girl touched me and it is okay because I make all things new! Jesus doesn't want us to stay how we are when He finds us. He wants us to become more like Him. We become more like Him when we get into His Word and read the red letters of His life. We become like Him when we lay down our religion and seek a relationship with Him. We cannot let our fears keep us from seeking that relationship.

Sometimes we need to take a risk in order to encounter our Lord. Sometimes we are going to look a little crazy when we step out of our comfort zones and do what our heart tells us to do. She had to take a risk of faith. She was desperate enough to take the risk. Are you desperate enough to be set free? Are you desperate enough to run into the arms of your Lord and encounter Him? What is getting in the way of running straight to Him? Pride? Your material possessions? An immoral relationship? Doubt? Insecurity? Cancer? Foreclosure?

Jesus will allow circumstances in our lives that will make us desperate for Him. We can get so caught up in the why would He allow this to happen to me that we will never encounter Him and allow Him to be our Savior. The bleeding woman could have easily stayed where she was, broken, unclean and rejected by everyone wondering why she had to suffer for 12 years and lose everything and she would have missed the opportunity to experience Him as Savior. Is that where you are? Are you chained to your circumstances? Are your circumstances going to get in the way of your encounter with the Savior?

John 8:1-11 The Message Jesus went across to Mount Olives, but He was soon back in the temple again. Swarms of people came to Him. He sat down and taught them.

The religion scholars and Pharisees led in a woman who had been caught in an act of adultery. They stood her in plain sight of everyone and said, "Teacher this woman was caught red-handed in the act of adultery. Moses, in the law gives orders to stone such persons. What do you say? They were trying to trap Him into saying something incriminating so they could bring charges against Him.

Jesus bent down and wrote with His finger in the dirt. They kept at Him, badgering Him. He straightened up and said, "The sinless one among you, go first: Throw the stone." Bending down again, He wrote some more in the dirt.

Hearing that, they walked away, one after another, beginning with the oldest. The woman was left alone. Jesus stood up and spoke to her. "Woman, where are they? Does no one condemn you?

No one, Master.

Neither do I, said Jesus. Go on your way. From now on don't sin.

A young woman caught in the very act of adultery. I just want you to try and put yourself in her shoes for a moment. We don't know for sure but I think she was probably caught in the moment in bed with a married man when the religious leaders pushed their way right into her bedroom. I can only assume but I am sure she was naked. From the reputation that we have come to know of these religious leaders I doubt that they allowed her to get herself together or even grab a robe to cover her bare body before they decided to drag her through the streets of her small town and throw her at the feet of Jesus. I can only imagine them dragging her kicking and screaming causing quite the scene.

Jesus was sitting amongst a group of people teaching but with the commotion of the woman being dragged through the streets it must have brought Him to His feet.

So there she is either naked or half covered, trembling in her guilt and shame as she is brought face to face with the only one who could save her. Here she is standing before the One who knows no sin. She must have felt dirty, unworthy to even stand in His Presence. I wonder if she even had wished the stoning had been over with.

The religious leaders plead their case to Jesus. They explain to Him of her unclean acts of adultery and they remind Him of the consequences of her sin. The consequence would be for the crowd to stone her to death. Our Lord as calm and humble as He is kneels to the ground and begins to write in the sand with His finger. The religious leaders won't let up so Jesus stands again and he utters the words, "those without sin must throw the first stone!" The broken woman must have let out a sigh of relief for we all know that no one is without sin. Jesus kneels back down again and goes back to His drawing in the sand. Then one by one as the conviction pierced their own hearts they left the scene until it was just the woman and Jesus. I can picture Him reaching out to her hands so He could pull her to her feet and staring straight into her eyes as He pulled her to her feet. He asks her, where have they gone, hasn't anyone condemned you? I am sure it was but with a whisper, she said No one sir. I love these words that He tells her, then neither do I, go now and leave your life of sin. She was face to face with her Savior and He set her free, He saved her from her sins with the request of leaving her life of sin behind her. He asked her to know Him as Lord. He asked her to lay aside her fleshly wants and desires. He asked her to lay down the sin that was getting in the way of their relationship. Do you think that she never committed another sin from that day forward? Just like the bleeding woman we don't know what happened after that encounter with Jesus but I highly doubt that she went back to that same bed and I guarantee that she was forever changed after that encounter with Jesus. She had come to Him broken, humiliated and unclean and she left Him forgiven and free!

Jesus accepts us no matter where we are in our lives even when we are caught in the very act of sin. Jesus takes us exactly where we are at, no matter what sin we are entangled in. He takes us with all of our hang ups, our mistakes, our guilt, our shame, our unbelief and our wrong motives. He looks at us with all of our stuff and He doesn't judge us, He reaches out His Hand and wants to walk down our path with us cleaning it up as we walk with Him. AMAZING, isn't it?

Sometimes just like the adulterous woman we need someone to carry us to Jesus' feet. So that person in your life who has been trying to share with you and get you to go to church that just may be the one He has chosen to carry you to His feet. Be vulnerable, open up and allow Jesus to move in your life. Sometimes we think we are just not worthy to sit at the Lord's Feet so we avoid Him and as we are avoiding him our chains just get heavier.

I pray and I hope that as sisters and brothers in Christ when we recognize one another enslaved in sin that we would bring our friends to the feet of Jesus. I pray that we would not bring them as the religious leaders did in judgment and with their own agenda but that we would do it in love and that we would help them in any way we can! Sometimes we don't have the strength to run to Jesus ourselves and we need to be carried and dropped off at His feet.

It doesn't matter what you have done. We have been so programmed to think that when we get right then we can go to God. I will get all cleaned up and then I can go to church and that is not how Jesus wants us to think. He wants you to know that it does not matter what you have done or where your feet have traveled He just wants you to come as you are and have an intimate relationship with Him.

Another story that has spoken volumes to me is the encounter with Jesus and Lazarus. This story is full of grieving, tragedy and then triumph. Mary, Martha and Lazarus were siblings that lived together in Bethany. Whenever Jesus was in Bethany this is who He would stay with. Lazarus has become ill and Mary and Martha know just who to get the message to, Jesus.

John 11:17-44 NLT When Jesus arrived at Bethany, He was told that Lazarus had already been in his grave for four days. Bethany was only a few miles down the road from Jerusalem and many of the people had come to console Martha and Mary in their loss. When Martha got word that Jesus was coming, she went to meet Him. But Mary stayed in the house. Martha said to Jesus, "Lord, if only you had been here, my brother would not have died. But even now I know that God will give you whatever you ask.

Jesus told her, "Your brother will rise again."

Yes, Martha said, "he will rise when everyone else rises, at the last day.

Jesus told her, "I am the resurrection and the life." Anyone who believes in Me will live, even after dying. Everyone who lives in Me and believes in Me will never die. Do you believe this, Martha?"

"Yes, Lord," she told him. "I have always believed you are the Messiah, the Son of God, the one who has come into the world from God." Then she left him and returned to Mary. She called Mary aside from the mourners and told her, "The Teacher is here and wants to see you." So Mary immediately went to him.

Jesus had stayed outside the village, at the place where Martha met him. When the people who were at the house trying to console Mary saw her leave so hastily, they assumed she was going to Lazarus's grave to weep. So they followed her there. When Mary arrived and saw Jesus, she fell down at his feet and said, "Lord, if you had been here, my brother would not have died."

When Jesus saw her weeping and saw the other people wailing with her, a deep anger welled up within Him and He was deeply troubled. "Where have you put him?" he asked them.

They told him, "Lord, come and see." Then Jesus wept. The people who were standing nearby said, "See how much he loved him." But some said, "This man healed a blind man. Why couldn't he keep Lazarus from dying?"

Jesus was still angry as He arrived at the tomb, a cave with a stone rolled across its entrance. "Roll the stone aside," Jesus told them.

But Martha, the dead man's sister, protested, "Lord, he has been dead for four days. The smell will be terrible."

Jesus responded, "Didn't I tell you that you will see God's glory if you believe?" So they rolled the stone aside. Then Jesus looked up to heaven and said, "Father, thank you for hearing me. You always hear me, but I said it out loud for the sake of all these people standing here, so they will believe you sent me." Then Jesus shouted, "Lazarus, come out!" And the dead man came out, his hands and feet bound in graveclothes, his face wrapped in a headcloth. Jesus told them, "Unwrap him and let him go!" Many of the people who were with Mary believed in Jesus when they saw this happen.

You may recall Martha and Mary from the gospel of Luke. Jesus has come for dinner and Martha is busy preparing the meal and setting the table making sure everything is just perfect for Jesus while her sister Mary can't seem to stay away from sitting at Jesus' feet listening to all that He has to say looking up at him worshipping her Lord.

Jesus receives the message that Lazarus is very sick from Mary and Martha and sends one back to them; Lazarus's sickness will not end in death. No it happened for the glory of God so that the Son of God will receive glory from this. Mary and

Martha feel better as they know that Jesus will come take care of their brother. But two days has passed and no Jesus. Lazarus becomes more ill and dies. Mary and Martha began to doubt Jesus, but you said he would not die Lord. I thought you would have been here by now to save my brothers life. There are times in our walk with Jesus too that we begin to doubt Him because He has us wait on an answer. Things don't look like the way we had planned them to. We have His Word. He has a plan and His plans for us are for good and not for disaster, He wants to give us a future and a hope. He knows what He is doing all the time and we do not. This is where we must trust Him and have faith. Jesus arrives in Bethany and Martha runs and greets him and bombards Him with her sorrow and her doubt. Lord if only you had been there he would still be alive. He assures her I am in control your brother will rise again. She is thinking with what she knows of the resurrection day when we will all rise but Jesus assures her that He is the resurrection and the life. Jesus asks for Mary and Martha runs to tell her sister that Jesus wants her. Mary without hesitating runs to Jesus and says the same thing to Him; Lord if only you had been here my brother would have not died. Jesus becomes very disturbed as He sees Mary weeping and He has a deep anger stir up inside Him. He asks where have you put him? Jesus wept. He feels our pain. He knows our grief and as He sees His dear friends mourning the death of their brother He mourns with them. That is Jesus your Lord. He mourns with you too. I also think He weeps because He knows He is about to bring Lazarus out of Paradise and back into a broken world where pain and suffering surround us.

Jesus tells them to roll the stone away. Once again Martha doubts Jesus but Lord he has been in there for four days the smell will be terrible. Jesus responds Didn't I tell you that you would see God's glory if you believe? They rolled the stone away and Jesus prayed out loud. Father thank you for hearing me. You always hear me but I say it out loud for the sake of all these people standing here so that they will believe you sent me. Then Jesus shouted Lazarus come out! Jesus was relying on the Father and His Power and He wanted the people to give God the glory for this miracle. Once again insisting that they believe and not doubt. Lazarus came out with his hands and feet bound in grave clothes. Jesus told them unwrap him and let him go.

There is a time when Jesus calls all of us by name and says Tiffany come out. Leave your life of sin and come and follow me. We too are bound in grave clothes from whatever sins have killed our soul. Jesus is calling our name and asking us to remove our grave clothes of sin. If you have never surrendered to Jesus and allowed Him to unwrap you from your life of sin today would be a great day to come out of the grave. Just say something like Jesus thank you for calling my name. I hear you and I want to come out of the grave of sin. Forgive me for what I have done wrong. Help me to unwrap my grave clothes from my life and help me to follow you the rest of my days. Thank you for dying on the cross for me and for giving me a new life. In your name I say this, Amen.

You may have already heard your name years ago but you have fallen into sin take today to Return to Him and repent. Take off your grave clothes of sin and allow Him to be New again in your life.

Each of these encounters all started with brokenness. The bleeding woman was physically broken. The adulterous woman was emotionally broken and through Lazarus death Mary and Martha were spiritually broken by doubt. Brokenness is beautiful to God because when we are broken whether it is physically, emotionally or spiritually we come to a place of surrender where we run to God because we have no where else to run. When we feel whole and things are running smoothly we tend to forget about God. God never forgets about us. God is always in control even when our circumstances seem out of control. God notices you. God knows every detail of your life and He cares deeply for you. He hurts when you hurt and He rejoices when you rejoice. I just can't say that enough. Just like these encounters He is waiting to have an encounter with you. We have the awesome opportunity of having an encounter with the Living God every day if we chose to.

We have all had circumstances in our lives whether it is a sickness like the bleeding woman, a choice to be unfaithful to our spouse and our Lord or choices that lead to death but we have a compassionate God that is waiting for us to rely on Him and encounter Him in our daily lives.

A State of the Heart

※

1 Samuel 16:7b NIV Man looks at the outward appearance but God looks at the heart.

Your heart is the center of who you are. Your heart makes you do the things that you do. What is the attitude of your heart? Jesus in Mark 7 recites some scriptures from Isaiah, *"These people honor me with their lips but their hearts are far away from me. Their worship is a farce, for they teach man-made ideas as commands from God. For you ignore God's law and substitute your own tradition. You skillfully sidestep God's law in order to hold onto your own tradition. Their traditions became more important than the scriptures."* In Mark 7 Jesus was addressing a group of religious leaders, the Pharisees. The Pharisees were the group who would later be the ones to crucify Jesus and it all began in their hearts.

We do the same thing as the religious leaders we honor God with our lips. We sing songs that say our hearts are surrendered and that we will follow Him wherever He leads and yet we run from the Lord when we hear His voice speak to our hearts. We are so programmed to make sure we are seen at church each week and show up to bible study, check off our list of service for the week that we have become religious. We as Christians are missing the mark. The states of our hearts have become religious.

This same heart issue completely turned me away from religion. I was raised in Catholicism. I am not here to bash Catholicism. I respect the religion. The religion taught me an awe and reverence to God. I stand in awe of the beautiful cathedrals that are built in the name of Jesus and they somehow gave me an awe factor of God. The priests and nuns made me feel as if I could never measure up to God's love. I felt like His love was based on my performance and it held me captive to performance and judgment. I was always concerned about my outer appearance and never really looked at my heart issues.

Pharisees are into religion. They follow the man made traditions and man made theology and Jesus warns us in Mark not to follow these man made traditions or religion. Religion keeps us away from God. These things will keep you away from Jesus. You will get caught up in following rules and traditions and you will miss God in this. Jesus is not into our religion. Jesus warned the Pharisees that they would cancel the Word of God just so that they could hand down the traditions. That's what religion does. We pass down the tradition of religion and we miss getting to know the true living God.

Pharisees are into receiving the glory. That is what stirred up the anger and the hate in their hearts towards Jesus. People were starting to follow Jesus. Their jealousy was growing because their followers were starting to follow Jesus and no longer following them. They were beginning to see that Jesus had compassion for them. He was willing to sit amongst them and dwell with them. He was willing to listen to them. They wanted to follow Him. They saw that they could have a relationship with Jesus not a religion. The Pharisees were jealous and they wanted to get rid of Jesus so that they could receive the glory again so that the people would come to them and bow down at their feet again.

Pharisees were worried about the outer appearance and completely neglected the inner purity that Jesus is after. *1 Samuel 16:7 NIV says But the Lord said to Samuel, "Don't judge by his appearance or height, for I have rejected him. The Lord doesn't see things the way you see them. People judge by the outward appearance but the Lord looks at the heart.*

When Jesus called Levi (who He would later be called Matthew) to be His disciple, Levi was a tax collector who would have been a social outcast and this got the religious leaders angry. Jesus not only called Levi to be His disciple but also spent the evening in his home with his friends who some were tax collectors and others disreputable sinners. In their words, Why would He eat with such scum? This statement alone shows the hearts of these religious leaders. They had hard hearts that had no compassion or love for anyone that did not follow their rules or bow down and worship them.

Unfortunately there are many religious leaders in the church today that have this same attitude and they have turned the people away from Jesus. It is time to take a good look into our religious hearts and allow Jesus to transform our hearts into hearts that follow Him. We need to get back to the Gospel message that Jesus came to share. Repent of whatever it is that you do that has you running away from God. Surrender your life and allow Him to turn your heart of stone into a heart of flesh.

I often wonder how Jesus would respond to our modern day Christianity? Are we like the Religious leaders? Are we acting like Jesus or like the religious leaders? Today at a gay/lesbian pride parade are we on the other side of the street with our picket signs that say the lies of God hates fags or gay men and lesbians are going to hell or are we there sharing Jesus with them? Maybe sitting down and seeing the gay man for the person that he is. These are God's children that are struggling with the sin of homosexuality. God hates sin and homosexuality is a sin just like my lying lips are a sin. I know my Lord and Savior would not be on the side of the street with the picket signs, Jesus Christ would be walking amongst them not agreeing with their choices but He would sit down and have dinner with them sharing them the freedom that they too can have through Him. He was found amongst the sinners.

We tend to look at the outer appearance and Jesus is only looking at our heart. He is the only one who can see inside our hearts. He knows where we are at and He knows where we have been and He knows where we are going to go. We need to do a heart check and see where we are in our walk? Are we looking at the outer appearance? What is in our own lives that we can be working on in our own hearts instead of looking at what others are doing? Our hearts are greedy and lustful. We want what we don't have in the things of this world. We are easily distracted and we get caught up in our earthly circumstances. The only person that we should be looking at or comparing ourselves to is Jesus Himself. The only way to get our hearts to have that inner purity is to learn the heart of Christ. We need to look at His heart and see that His heart is pure. He was always ready to forgive even when He was betrayed. Jesus' heart was peaceful. His heart was not anxious. His heart was after His Father in Heaven's Heart. He was looking to God to get His next assignment. His Heart was moldable and it was ready to be obedient. His heart listened for the voice of His Father.

Jesus is interested in the care of people. He is interested in you being transformed from the inside out. He is not interested in how well you follow the law. He does not want outer works of service until your heart has been cleaned out and transformed. He wants you to love the Lord your God with all of your heart and then you will be open and listening for His next assignment for you. Jesus doesn't show up to church to see what clothes you have on or if you brought your bible to church He is looking at our heart. He wants to penetrate the heart. He wants to go deep into the roots of bitterness and anger that cause us to sin and separate us from Him every day and He wants to rip them out and replace them with His Love and His Mercy.

We have created a religion of Christianity. That is never what God intended for us. God wants to have a personal intimate relationship with each one of us. He wants to change us from the inside out. I once again will remind you of *Amos 5:21-24 The Message I can't stand your religious meetings. I'm fed up with your conferences and conventions. I want nothing to do with your religious projects, your pretentious slogans and goals. I'm sick of your fund raising schemes, your public relations and image making. I've had all I can take of your noisy ego-music. When was the last time you sang to me? Do you know what I want? I want justice-oceans of it. I want fairness-rivers of it. That's what I want. That's all I want!* You see God is not interested in the next big building we can build or the next conference on how to be a better Christian. He wants our hearts. He wants to be involved in our lives. How many times did He warn the Pharisees and Religious Leaders to stop judging people by what they did or what nationality they were? Jew or Gentile? Rich or poor? Leper or not? He doesn't want us to make Him an image. He already created us in His Image and now He wants us to grow to know Him so that we can act like Him. What does God want? He wants to hear your voice talking to Him! He wants to see us standing up for the things that He would stand up for. He wants justice-oceans of it. He wants fairness….that is His Heart. What we have done in and to this world breaks His Heart. He wants the world to be right the way He created it to be PERFECT! And yet He waits so patiently so that everyone would have a chance to know Him as Lord. It is up to us. It is our choice to believe in Him! He wants your heart and He wants it completely.

It is time to surrender our religious beliefs, our idols, our attitudes and our hearts. It is time to surrender our false expectations of how God does things or who God is. It is time to lay down our spiritual pride.

When we surrender our hearts to the Lord we become new. Our filth is washed away and HE remembers our sin no more. We become flooded in God's Grace. God's Grace is His undeserved favor over our lives. It no longer depends on what we do to earn God's love. It's not about our performance or our dedication to God for Him to show kindness.

Isaiah 57:15 The high and lofty one who lives in eternity, the Holy One, says this: I live in the high and holy place with those whose spirits are contrite and humble. I restore the crushed spirit of the humble and revive the courage of those with repentant hearts.

We need to get down off our high and lofty places of success and how great we think we are and bow before our Maker.

This world has programmed us into thinking in a temporal way. We have temporal attitudes in our hearts and yet our spirits know that there has to be something more than this. We have an unsettled spirit within us that knows this isn't our home. Life is good here most of the time. I am blessed, you are blessed. We work hard and we accumulate things of this world but at the end of the day if we haven't connected with our Creator then our day was meaningless. We feel empty. We need to surrender our hearts and our attitudes to Jesus.

When we return to Jesus and keep our eyes on Him then we are complete. We lack nothing. We need to surrender our hearts to Him. How do we surrender our hearts to Him? One day at a time. He is eager to relent and not punish. He wants us to approach Him with repentant hearts which in turn opens up an intimate relationship with Him. The only thing that gets in the way of our relationship with God is sin. Repentance is the answer. Repentance is to turn from sin and change one's heart and behavior. We have to do this one day at a time. His mercies are new every morning and they are available to us. We are sinners and we will fall but when we are in an intimate relationship with the Father and our hearts are His we won't want to stray very far. We will recognize when we have sinned and we will repent. His kindness leads us to repentance. He is filled with unfailing love and is more than willing to forgive us our sins when we confess them and ask for forgiveness.

Joel 2:12 NIV Even now declares the Lord, return to Me with all your heart, with fasting and weeping and mourning. He wants us to turn from our sin and return to Him with all our heart. Fast from your sin. Weep about your sin. Know that it is wrong what we are doing and mourn about our sin. When we do give our hearts to God we will recognize what is wrong in our lives and we will turn away from the sins that so easily entangle us and we will return to Him. God is always promising to restore whatever we have lost when we turn away from our sin and we return our hearts to Him.

Sometimes sin hides in our hearts. We may have had our feelings hurt and never chose to forgive and then a root of bitterness takes place in our hearts and sin follows after bitterness. We need to get to the same place that David reached in his heart. *Psalm 139:23-24 NLT Search me O God and know my heart; test me and know my anxious thoughts. Point out anything that offends You, and lead me along the path of everlasting life.* When we get to this place and we surrender our hearts to God and invite Him into our hearts completely then He has the chance to reveal to us what needs to be cleaned out. We can wake up each morning and invite Him into our hearts showing what needs to be changed for that day. He may reveal things to you that you didn't even realize you struggled with but He is there to walk through it with you every step of the way.

Jeremiah 24:7 NIV I will give them hearts that recognize Me as the Lord. They will be My people and I will be their God, for they will return to Me wholeheartedly. This is the verse that inspired me to write this book. It is time to start looking at our hearts with an eternal view in mind not this temporal world that we focus on. As we keep our eyes fixed on Jesus and eternity our hearts will return to Him wholeheartedly and God can be our God. What is the state of your heart?

Everyday Worship

≈

1 John 5:21 NLT Dear children, keep away from anything that might take God's place in your hearts.

I am always fascinated with the Israelites because as I read through story after story about them in the Old Testament I sit scratching my head wondering how they could have been so impatient and well stupid! They were all about grumbling, complaining and they were very ungrateful. In just three months God had revealed Himself to them in numerous ways. He parted the Red Sea to deliver them from the Egyptians. They were hungry and He provided manna to fall from the sky to feed them. They were thirsty and He provided water to flow from a rock. They were lost so He came at night in a pillar of fire and during the day He guided them in the clouds. He showed up. He provided. He was faithful.

We too are so impatient and stupid. We are just like the Israelites in so many ways. We have a God who is chasing after us with His Grace and we grumble and complain that we are bored. We want more stuff. What we have is just not enough and we like the Israelites end up building and setting up idols in our lives. Let's take a look at a story in Exodus

32. Moses has gone on the mountain top to meet with God. The Israelites were told to wait down below for him to return. Moses was just taking too long and the Israelites were getting impatient. They were bored. They approach Moses brother Aaron and start complaining, "Come on make us gods who can lead us. Moses is not coming back. We don't know what happened to that fellow Moses that brought us out of Egypt but we don't care because even though he delivered us from the slavery we were in Egypt he brought us out into the middle of the desert to eat the same food over and over again and we are bored so forget about him. Make us something we can see and touch." So Aaron out of fear tells them to gather the gold rings from everyone. He then melts all the gathered gold and creates a golden calf. Immediately the people are so excited and without hesitation start to worship the golden calf. They have created a new deliverer, a new savior. Really? A golden calf? It is a statue that they would rather worship than wait for Moses who has delivered them, who rescued them from slavery and who they saw God work miracles through. They were so excited they had something to worship. Aaron saw the excitement in the people so he builds an altar for the calf and they decide to have a festival to the Lord and worship the calf in the morning. The Israelites forgot their boredom along with their God and began to prepare their burnt offerings and peace offerings to the gold calf.

Now reading that we can sit and think why would you worship a gold statue of a cow and leave your God that has just delivered you from slavery? Wrestling with Idolatry is something every human heart struggles with. Ezekiel 14:3 says the leaders set up idols in their hearts. They have embraced things that will make them fall into sin. An idol is anything that will take God's place in our hearts. We can fall into idolatry so easily and we do it everyday.

We do the same thing as the Israelites. We get bored, we create our own gods and we worship idols. Idols are anything that distracts us from going to God first. We these days worship knowledge of stuff more than we go to God. We worship money and material things. We worship success and our big houses with the white picket fences. We worship sex and our bodies. We worship drugs and alcohol to ease the burdens of this life. We have created our own golden cows. We got bored. We got tired of waiting on God to deliver us from our depression or our financial struggle. Our marriages are falling apart and our children are turning prodigal but we don't turn to God we turn to shopping and a glass of wine. We just like the Israelites can fall into the trap of Idolatry on any given day when we take our eyes off of Jesus just like they took their eyes off of God.

Who or what do you run to when you get bored? Do you run to the mall and go shopping? Do you run to the refrigerator and the cupboard to fill yourself up with carbs? Maybe you run to the TV to get lost in the not so real world of television. Do you go to the gym because you are so obsessed with your body to look like hers or his? Do you go down to the nearest pub where everybody knows your name? These are temporary band aids to wounds we have or circumstances that we are going through. They are our idols.

In the very first book of the Bible in the beginning of time we broke God's heart with idolatry. Adam and Eve decided that they would worship an idol. The idol of pride and selfishness. Having everything complete and perfect was not good enough for her. She was curious. She began to doubt that God had her best in sight. She began to question if God was really for her and not against her? Why had He forbidden the fruit from the Tree of Life? I must be good enough to eat of its fruit. We do the same thing today. We are just not sure if God can handle our life. We are not sure if He will come through the way we want Him to. We seem to think that we know a little more than He does and we can make far better choices for our family, our spouse and our careers. People back then lived to please themselves rather than their Creator and we too live for ourselves and forget so quickly about our Creator.

God wants to be the One we run to when are lacking something. He wants to be the one that we go to when we are bored. He is the one that knows us better than we know ourselves. He also wants us to make Him the one we run to by our own choice. He will never force us to love Him and He will never force us to choose Him.

These idols here are temporary and this life goes by in the blink of an eye so if we choose to look at all the stuff here and worship it we will find ourselves very empty not only here but on the other side of eternity.

Aren't you tired of chasing the American Dream? Aren't you tired of keeping the perfect house? Aren't you tired of trying to raise the perfect kids with perfect grades to go to the perfect college that will teach them to hate God? Aren't you tired of keeping up with the latest trends and fashions? Our idols will exhaust us. They can't give anything back to us. They only take from us. Make a commitment to being in His Word daily allowing Him to transform you from the inside out.

Because we cannot see God it makes it hard for us to believe in Him. There are things all around us every day that promise to make us successful, beautiful and more spiritual but none of these things can save us. Money, beauty, success are all good things. We need money to live. We want to be beautiful to someone and to be successful at our career so that we can provide for our family right? Yes these are all good things but it is when these good things become all we can concentrate on that they become bad. It is when our lives revolve around these good things. We need to repent of all that keeps us from making God first in our hearts. Repent means to turn away from your idol and return to the Living God.

It is time for us to face the reality of our spiritual conditions. Jesus said, "Love the Lord your God with all your heart, all your soul and all your mind." When we have idols overflowing in our hearts there is no room to love the Lord our God with all our hearts so today as 1 *John 5:21 NLT says,"Dear children, keep away from anything that might take God's place in your hearts."* So what does it mean to love the Lord your God with all your heart?

Romans 12:1-2 The Message

So here's what I want you to do, God helping you: Take your everyday, ordinary life-your sleeping, eating, going-to-work, and walking around life- and place it before God as an offering. Embracing what God does for you is the best thing you can do for Him. Don't become so well adjusted to your culture that you fit into it without even thinking. Instead, fix your attention on God. You'll be changed from the inside out. Readily recognize what He wants from you, and quickly respond to it. Unlike the culture around you, always dragging you down to its level of immaturity, God brings the best out of you, develops well-informed maturity in you.

When we think of sacrifices and offerings we think of the dead animals that the people of the Old Testament used to have to leave at the altar and offer to God for forgiveness for their sins. Paul is telling us that our lives are now the living sacrifice that we need to offer God. We are a holy sacrifice not because of who we are or what we do but because of who Jesus is and what He did for us on the cross 2000 years ago. The problem with being a living sacrifice is that we can crawl right off that altar of sacrifice which is why we have to give Him our lives everyday. How do we live a life of worship everyday of our life? How do we keep our eyes on Jesus and not look to idols in our life for comfort? We have to choose to love Him with all of our hearts. We have to give ourselves to God. He is an intimate God who knows us intimately and He wants us to know Him intimately back. By giving God access to us completely we can have that intimate relationship with Him. Our lives are to be a living sacrifice. We have to keep our minds on the Lord everyday! Romans 12:2 says do not copy the behaviors of this world. We live in this world but we are not of this world and that is why we need to daily surrender our lives to God and allow Him to change us from the inside out through His Word and with the help of the Holy Spirit as He convicts us of things we should avoid in this world that will take our eyes off of Jesus and get us copying the behaviors and customs of this world. Create ways everyday that will help you remember what Jesus has done for you. I listen to worship music all the time not just on Sundays at church and it keeps my eyes on Jesus. Your bible should be a part of your every day worship. God's Word is alive and active and it pierces our thoughts and actions. We need to know what His Word says! It is not hard to follow hard after God it is a choice to follow Him hard everyday!

God has always chosen ordinary people to do extraordinary things for Him. In Hebrews there is a hall of faith that includes ordinary people that put their faith in an extraordinary God and they did extraordinary things. By faith Noah built an ark on dry land and saved his family. Noah was the only one left on the planet that still believed in God. Can you imagine the bullying that he would have endured? But God saw his heart and He allowed Noah to be the second father of the human race. He put a God sized dream in Noah's heart. Genesis 6:22 Noah did everything just as God had commanded him to. He had faith. He gave His life as a living sacrifice. He endured the ridicule and he turned his cheek to the humiliation that was felt as person after person would come by and tell him how stupid he was for believing in God and building an ark. Noah wasn't perfect. God made sure to include his night of drunkenness and embarrassing himself in front of his sons not to humiliate Noah but to show us He uses ordinary people that make mistakes to do extraordinary God-sized things.

By faith, Moses left the privileges of the Egyptian Royal house to a hard life with God's people. His life was a living sacrifice. His eyes were on God. Moses in his weakness chose to follow God and obey God. He was afraid to speak. He stuttered. How was he going to deliver the Israelites from the Egyptians? Moses an ordinary guy did extraordinary God sized things. God molded Moses weaknesses and made them work for His purpose.

By faith Mary a teenage girl surrendered her life to God and had the privilege of being the mother of God's son. She was just a young girl that God had found favor with. She had an angel come to her and tell her that God would place His Son in her womb and she would be His Sons mother. Her response was, I am the Lord's servant. May everything you have said about me come true. She offered her body as a living sacrifice. Mary was just an ordinary girl with an extraordinary heart.

By faith Peter was the first strong voice for the Gospel. Peter was harsh and abrasive. He was compulsive and did everything without thinking. He always spoke without thinking. Peter denied Jesus three times during his trial and suffered greatly emotionally from that denial. After he repented and rededicated his life to Jesus he surrendered his life a living sacrifice and was able to build the church and lead many straight to Jesus heart. Peter knew His unfaithfulness could never take away God's faithfulness to him. Peter was an ordinary guy who surrendered and did extraordinary things for God.

By faith Paul wrote most of the New Testament. He went from persecuting Christians to saving people for Jesus. Paul was the poster child for religion until he met Jesus face to face. He realized that it was all about a relationship with Jesus and this transformed his thoughts, his actions and his life. Absolutely amazing what Jesus can do with someone when they take their ordinary life and give it to an extraordinary God.

These are just a few of the ordinary people that God has allowed us to see in His Word. There are many other stories in the bible of life after life being transformed by an extraordinary God when we allow ourselves to give Him our everyday worship. Loving God with all our heart will lead to doing some extraordinary things for Him and His Kingdom. It is not about religion or a list of rules to follow. It is not a to do list where you get to check off going to church for the week or reading your bible for the day but an every day act of laying our lives down on God's altar and allowing Him to love people through us. It is about us being obedient to God not to earn a relationship with God but to have a relationship with God. *1 John 5:21 NLT Dear children, keep away from anything that might take God's place in your hearts.* If you want to do God sized things and step out of your ordinary life then keep away from anything that might take God's place in your heart.

Getting Ready For Forever

≈

1 Corinthians 2:9 NIV No eye has seen, no ear has heard, no mind has conceived what God has prepared for those who love Him.

1 Corinthians 1:18-25 NLT The message of the cross is foolish to those who are headed for destruction! But we who are being saved know it is the very power of God. As the scriptures say, "I will destroy the wisdom of the wise and discard the intelligence of the intelligent." So where does this leave the philosophers, the scholars, and the worlds brilliant debaters? God has made the wisdom of this world look foolish. Since God in His wisdom saw to it that the world would never know Him through human wisdom, He has used our foolish preaching to save those who believe. It is foolish to the Jews who ask for signs from heaven. And it is foolish to the Greeks who seek human wisdom. So when we preach that Christ was crucified, the Jews are offended and the Gentiles say it is all nonsense. But to those called by God to salvation, both Jews and Gentiles, Christ is the power of God and the wisdom of God. This foolish plan of God is wiser than the wisest of human plans, and God's weakness is stronger than the greatest of human strength.

For most of my life I misunderstood what the cross meant and misunderstood who Jesus was. It was as if I had earplugs in my ears and a veil over my eyes. The cross sounded foolish. I can only say that today the more that I study the cross and study the life of Jesus the more power I have in my life. Jesus is the power to walk in this world with freedom and confidence. He is the answer to every problem. Faith is the key ingredient needed here. The bible says the cross sounds foolish to those who don't believe. I know I have been there before trying to figure it all out but it was only when I invited God into my life to reveal Himself to me that the cross began to make sense. I was at my lowest point in my life when I had tried everything else to make me happy. I had tried relationships, numbing myself with alcohol and I was on my own making my decisions and I was going nowhere fast. I was a single mom with a beautiful 3 year old son and I was pregnant again. I was too selfish to have another baby and put that kind of pressure on me to support two kids so I decided to get an abortion. I swore I would never do that as I would hear of friends that were making that choice but it seemed hopeless at the time and I made the appointment as soon as possible in fear I would change my mind. I went to the appointment I stood in line and then it was my turn and it was over just like that. I went home and life goes on right? Life would go on but I knew I would never be the same. I had a hole in my heart that was beyond repair. I remember walking into the bathroom, closing the door behind me falling to my knees with the feelings of guilt and shame overwhelming me. All I could do was cry out for forgiveness. I wished I could rewind the day. I wished I was still pregnant. As I lay sobbing on the cold bathroom floor I felt an overwhelming sense of peace, it is the Peace that transcends all understanding. I couldn't even understand it as it was happening. The only way I can describe it is I felt like I had crawled into my daddy's lap and his arms were wrapped so tightly around me and I felt safe just as I did as a little girl whenever I was scared. Only this time this Comfort and Peace was different. It was bigger. I just kept hearing this still small voice saying that everything was going to be okay. I forgive you and I love you! Somehow on that cold bathroom floor I felt the power of God's justice and His love meet and become one and that one is Jesus. Jesus came right to me when I could not take another step on my own. He knows us so deeply and intimately that He knows when to invade our soul. He knows when we are ready to receive Him. He comes and meets us in an intimate and personal way. That is why it is so hard to find Him in religion because religion is cold and rigid and there is no room for God there. Somehow in the darkest time of my life God showed me who He truly is and that He is full of love and mercy and that His mercies are new for me and you every morning. God did not wait for me to get my life all together and then comfort me. He came to me when I was the most broken in my life. He followed me all the days of my life and invaded my soul when I allowed Him to. That day when I allowed Him into my life I began to prepare myself for forever.

I don't know if you have had an encounter with Jesus but if you haven't my prayer is that you would open your heart and allow Him to show you who He is. Revelation 3:20 says He is a gentleman and He will stand at the door and knock but He won't come in until He is invited in. He is not pushy. He does not want to control you with rules and regulations. He wants a relationship with you. He wants to be involved in your everyday life. He wants to be a part of your everyday worship. He wants your heart. He wants to be your example as a life lived with freedom. He wants to use this time you have on earth to get you ready for forever. Jesus is not concerned about what church you go to or how much money you give Him, He wants your heart, your whole heart.

People ask me all the time, "How do know that this is the right way to heaven?" "How do you know that Jesus is real?" My answer is always, I gave Jesus a chance and I invited Him into my life and I am forever changed. I feel Him with me everyday and He has changed me from the inside out. I don't think like I used to think. I read His Word and I know He is real. That hasn't always been the case. There was a time in my life when I would read the bible and it was like reading Chinese. That was before I opened my heart and allowed Jesus into my life.

If I am wrong than I guess my body will go into the ground and that will be it. Life will be over. But if I am right (I know that I am right) I will spend eternity with a loving God in a perfect world forever. You see I win either way.

But to those that reject their salvation in Jesus because of pride or foolishness you will spend eternity in hell. Hell is a place where you will feel like you're the only one who made it there in bitterness, darkness and agony for eternity. There is no reason for anyone to go to hell. Salvation is a free gift from God it just takes a little faith on this side of eternity. It doesn't take your good deeds or how well you did things on earth it only takes believing in Jesus.

No other god that is worshipped on this planet came to live amongst His people so that He could relate in every way possible to His kids. No other god suffered a horrific death so that He could pay for every sin ever committed. No other god was beaten beyond recognition for you. No other god was nailed to a cross naked and exposed in the most humiliating way for you. No other god is interested in you. No other god wants to have a personal relationship with you. Jesus paid it all! Jesus came down to earth to save us from ourselves.

It is your choice. God offers everyone His free gift of salvation there is nothing but faith required. *Romans 10:9-10 NLT If you confess with your mouth that Jesus is Lord and believe in your heart that God raised Him from the dead you will be saved. For it is by believing in your heart that you are made right with God and it is by confessing with your mouth that you are saved.* It has absolutely nothing to do with how good you are as a person. Good works do nothing to get you into heaven.

In order for us to be ready for forever we need to be reading God's Word. You need to be reading it for yourself. *Hebrews 4:12 NLT For the Word of God is alive and powerful. It is sharper than the sharpest two-edged sword, cutting between soul and spirit, between joint and marrow. It exposes our innermost thoughts and desires.* The bible is not just another book. It is God's love story for us and has story after story of His pursuit of His children. It has the unending message of His cry out to us to "RETURN" to Him and allow Him to protect us and guide us. The Old Testament has just as many stories of His love as the New Testament. The bible will change your life and your relationship with God. I have discovered that the whole book is tied together. You have to discover it for yourself. Allow yourself to be open to what is inside it.

There has to be more than this life. We go round and round trying to accumulate one more thing to make us happy. We have moments that are great here don't we? We have days that are just amazing, like our wedding day, the birth of our children and accomplishments that we achieve here on earth with diplomas and degrees but this life will go by in the blink of an eye. We have a whole lot of time in eternity. It is forever so shouldn't we be preparing ourselves for that?

I don't know the last time that you thought about eternity but eternity is forever. It is hard for us to imagine what forever is like because life as we know it ends. Relationships as we know them end. Flowers die, grass withers and our bodies return to the earth as dust. When we think of heaven we often think how boring it will be to sit on a cloud and play a harp forever. *1 Corinthians 2:9 NLT No eye has seen, no ear has heard, no mind has conceived what God has prepared for those who love Him.* WOW! We cannot even imagine with our earthly minds how awesome it will be in heaven. I do know that you are not going to want to miss the celebration that takes place for eternity. I dare you to imagine life without disease, without war, without hate, without pain and without tears. We will be without flaw. We will eat and we will know each other. We have eternity to catch up on all the stuff we just did not have time for here on this side.

John 14: 2 NLT In my Father's house are many rooms; if it were not so I would have told you. I am going there to prepare a place for you. God created our world in six days but Jesus returned to heaven 2000 years ago to go and prepare a place for His children for Eternity. He knows everything that you like and He is preparing your place in heaven to fulfill you for Eternity. No eye has seen all that God has prepared for those who love Him. You don't want to miss this party, I promise.

Are you getting ready for forever? Are you prepared for forever? My prayer is that you would take an honest look at this book and you would ponder Him in your heart and Return to Him with your whole heart. It is time to get down on your knees, get naked before God and allow Him to show you what has gotten in the way of you and Him! What have you put in the way of your relationship with Him? What needs to be removed in order for you to return to Him? Is it an idol? Is it bitterness in your heart? Is it religion? Is it pride? Only you and the Lord can work this one out.

Once we return to Him and allow Him to be the King of our lives reigning on the throne of our hearts all other things fall into place and you will never know this until you try it. Give Him a chance in your hearts! You will need three things…you will need prayer, His Word and an open and willing heart to give to Him.

Jeremiah 24:7 NIV I will give them hearts that recognize Me as their Lord. They will be my people, and I will be their God, for they will return to Me wholeheartedly. Today is a great day to trade in your old heart of stone for a new heart of flesh and allow God to move in your life! *Ezekiel 11:19-20 NLT And I will give them singleness of heart and put a new spirit within them. I will take away their stony, stubborn heart and give them a tender, responsive heart so they will obey my decrees and regulations. Then they will truly be my people and I will be their God.*

With Gratitude

≫≪

Return To Me. I finally finished something that I started.

Thank you Matthew, my knight in shining armor, for being Jesus to me and our four sons. You are constantly interceding for us and showing us a true example of Jesus' love and patience. Thank you for encouraging me every day that I could do this! I love you with all of my heart.

My four sons, Anthony, Jacob, Noah and Mason, thank you for helping me keep it real. You are all my favorites! Thanks for understanding when Mom was busy writing.

Ruthie Thune, thank you for the countless coffee times or lunch meetings where our mentor relationship turned into true friendship. Thank you for sharing your wisdom with me. You truly are a Proverbs 31 woman that I strive to be daily. Thank You! You are my spiritual mama!

To all my girlfriends, (you know who you are) thank you for the constant encouragement to keep pressing on. Without your constant support I would have quit. Thank you for the prayers, the laughter, the tears and the hours of just trying to be more like Jesus. I am so thankful to God for my girlfriends, my sister chicks! A special thank you to Amy…Thank you for lighting the fire in my heart to love Jesus! I love you!

To my mom and dad, thank you for being you so that I could be me. You two are my rock and have always been there for me and I love you!

All Glory to Him, now and forever Amen!